Political Cartoons from the Crash to the Millennium

HERBLOCK'S HISTORY

D1597556

Political Cartoons from the Crash to the Millennium

HERBLOCK'S HISTORY

"The Cartoon," Copyright 1977, 2000 by Herbert Block. Cartoons appear courtesy of Herbert Block. All rights reserved.

This catalogue accompanies the exhibition *Herblock's History: Political Cartoons from the Crash to the Millennium* in the Thomas Jefferson Building of the Library of Congress from October 17, 2000, to February 17, 2001.

The exhibition and catalogue were prepared with funds provided by the Caroline and Erwin Swann Memorial Fund for Caricature and Cartoon. The Swann Fund supports an ongoing program at the Library of Congress of preservation, publication, exhibition, acquisition, and scholarly research in the related fields of cartoon, caricature, and illustration.

Cover: Detail from *National-security blanket,* May 27, 1973 (75)

ISBN: 0-8444-1028-4

CONTENTS

7   Preface by James Billington

11   Herblock's History by Harry L. Katz

19   The Cartoon by Herbert Block

29   Portfolio of Herblock Cartoons

56   Exhibition Checklist

63   Select Bibliography

64   Credits

PREFACE

From before the stock market crash in 1929 through the new millennium
beginning in the year 2000, editorial cartoonist Herb Block has chronicled
the nation's political history, caricaturing twelve American presidents from
Herbert Hoover to Bill Clinton. He has received three Pulitzer Prizes for
editorial cartooning (1942, 1954, and 1979) and a fourth with *Washington
Post* colleagues for public service during the Watergate investigation (1973).
He is a Fellow of the American Academy of Arts and Sciences and in 1994
was awarded the Presidential Medal of Freedom. Earlier this year the Library
of Congress named him a "Living Legend" in recognition of his extraordinary
contributions to the nation. Numerous honorary degrees from institutions
nationwide, most recently a 1999 Doctor of Arts from Harvard University,
suggest academia has forgiven him for leaving college early to pursue a
career as an editorial cartoonist. And well it should, for no single cartoonist
or commentator in America has done more to educate and inform the public
during the past seven decades than Herb Block.

It is my great pleasure, as a friend and admirer, to introduce this first
exhibition of his original drawings in fifty years. *Herblock's History*
celebrates his gift to the Library of Congress of more than one hundred
works, spanning seventy years of world history and the astonishing breadth
of his distinguished career. Political cartoons represent the freedom of
expression inherent in American democracy, echoing the Library of
Congress's Bicentennial theme: "Libraries, Creativity, and Liberty."

On the cusp of a new millennium, Herb Block's drawings forcefully bring back the principal issues and events that shaped our world during the past century.

The sign of a great cartoonist is the ability to effect change, and Herb Block has influenced politicians and altered public opinion throughout his career. He coined the phrase "McCarthyism," effectively challenging the excesses of the anticommunist campaigns of the late 1940s and early 1950s. He followed Richard Nixon's political path from his House reelection campaign in 1950 to his resignation as president of the United States in 1974. He documented the Cold War from its inception after World War II to the collapse of the Soviet Union in 1994. Furthermore, his numerous powerful cartoons on poverty, race relations, and education not only express his personal commitment to civil rights but measure over time the nation's response to such issues.

In tens of thousands of drawings published in newspapers over the years, Herb Block has offered trenchant graphic commentary on virtually every notable incident and public figure from the Depression forward, portraying our history from his usually prescient, sometimes tragic, often funny, and always intelligent perspective. His drawings are his legacy, a monumental contribution to the profession of journalism and to future understanding of the times in which we live. The Library takes great pride in preserving them for posterity on behalf of the American people.

James H. Billington
The Librarian of Congress

"THIS IS THE FOREST PRIMEVAL——"

First daily cartoon
Chicago Daily News
April 24, 1929

"This is the forest primeval—"
April 24, 1929
Reproduction of original drawing
Published in the *Chicago Daily News* (1)

Concern for the depletion of our natural resources is not new. In his first daily cartoon, Herb Block deplored the clear-cutting of America's virgin forests and foreshadowed the economic wasteland to come in the next decade. The caption is the first line of Henry Wadsworth Longfellow's *Evangeline*.

Born in Chicago on October 13, 1909, Herbert Block grew up in a family where art, history, and politics really mattered. His father, an accomplished chemist, also had a talent for writing and cartooning, contributing to such turn-of-the-twentieth-century humor magazines as *Life, Puck,* and *Judge.* He also supported his son's early studies at the Art Institute of Chicago. He "showed me something about drawing," Herb Block says. His father also had worked as a reporter for the *Chicago Record* and Herb's older brother Bill was a reporter on the *Chicago Tribune* and later the *Chicago Sun.* During high school Herb Block drew cartoons and wrote a weekly column for the school newspaper. From his earliest years, he prepared for a career as a journalist.

After graduation from high school he worked briefly as a police reporter for Chicago's City News Bureau. He also wrote frequent paragraphs on topical subjects for a contributors' column in the *Tribune.* Becase pen names were common then, his father suggested combining two names into one, and "Herblock" was born. Enrolling at Lake Forest College in Illinois, he majored in English and political science, studying under a professor who had worked for the Secretariat of the League of Nations. Talks with this professor furthered his interest in international affairs. Near the end of his sophomore year, he applied for a job at the *Chicago Daily News,* which offered him a tryout to replace an editorial cartoonist who was leaving. The tryout worked so well that it ended his academic career.

Just nineteen in 1929, Herb Block joined the major leagues of newspaper

cartoonists. Among these were veteran *Chicago Tribune* cartoonists who
had not long before generously taken time to look at his school paper efforts,
discussed them with him, and given him originals of their drawings. Among
these established cartoonists were Carey Orr, Gaar Williams and the much-
loved and highly respected John T. McCutcheon, a Chicago institution.
Herb Block was a particular fan of "Ding" Darling of the *New York Herald
Tribune,* whose cartoon opinions were characterized by humor and vitality.
Others were Edmund Duffy of the *Baltimore Sun,* whose crayon drawings
were striking, and *Chicago News* colleague and front-page cartoonist,
Vaughn Shoemaker, whose work was noted for its clean pen lines. He
drew from them all in refining a style that remains to this day clear, concise,
and compelling.

Early in 1933, as Franklin Delano Roosevelt took office amid economic
devastation, Herb Block left the *Chicago News,* hired as the only editorial
cartoonist for the Newspaper Enterprise Association (NEA), a Scripps-
Howard feature service headquartered in Cleveland, Ohio. "The Cleveland
job was a whole new ball game," writes Herb Block in his memoirs. His
Chicago News cartoons had been syndicated nationally but now reached
a much larger number of papers. His commentary grew sharper and more
prescient through the 1930s, responding to widespread unemployment and
poverty in American and the concurrent rise of Fascism in Europe and
communist tyranny in the Soviet Union.

The Depression politicized Herb Block. Sheltered from economic
hardships by his steady income, he observed the suffering around him and
used his editorial panel as a vehicle for progressive reform. He admired
Franklin Delano Roosevelt's New Deal policies and recalls that "during the
early days of the New Deal I did get to see what government could do." Herb
Block came into his own then, stirring domestic controversy with powerful
images attacking the volatile oratory of such American demagogues as Father
Coughlin and Huey Long. Largely supportive of New Deal policies, he
nonetheless questioned President Roosevelt's efforts in some areas, notably

an unsuccessful attempt in 1937 to increase the number of Supreme
Court justices.

In foreign affairs he hit his stride, warning of the threats to peace posed
by Fascism in Europe. He created derisive portrayals of military dictators
Adolf Hitler, Benito Mussolini, and Francisco Franco scheming and dreaming
of conquests and empires. And he brought their activities to the notice of a
public and politicians who, after the disillusionment that followed World
War I, had turned inward to isolationism. Targeting dictatorships, Herb Block
used symbols to carry his art and his message: a sharpened Soviet sickle
poised to execute political prisoners or a Nazi cap extinguishing the lamp
of German civilization.

Herb Block was an early advocate of aid to the allies resisting Nazi
aggression, and he was for measures to prepare America for what was
becoming a great world struggle. He noted Nazi outrages, giving them
graphic form and visual power. He drew metaphors for the resilience of the
human spirit, the inhumanity of war, and the duplicity of dictators, finding
heroes among innocents and victims and taking to task villainous politicians.
By 1941, with Britain under siege by the Nazis and the Japanese attack on
Pearl Harbor still on the horizon, Herb Block's cartoons took aim at the
Rome-Berlin-Tokyo Axis.

Fred Ferguson, president of NEA, opposed what he called the cartoonist's
"interventionism" and what Herb Block called "anti-isolationism." Ferguson
summoned him to New York in spring 1942 to discuss their differences.
"My life has been full of fortunate coincidences," Herb Block has said, for,
even as he sat in the New York office awaiting the disagreeable face-off,
he received the news he had won his first Pulitzer Prize, vaulting him into
national prominence and leaving his flummoxed publisher speechless. His
1942 Pulitzer Prize, based on cartoons of 1941, vindicated Herb Block's
stance and solidified his reputation as one of the country's foremost
political commentators.

In early 1943, he was drafted into the Army at the age of 33. He produced cartoons and articles and edited a "clipsheet" that was distributed throughout the Army, until he was mustered out of the service in late 1945.

He moved to Washington, hired as editorial cartoonist by the *Washington Post* to begin work at the start of 1946. He has remained in that position ever since, drawing daily cartoons from the nation's capital for more than half a century. Katharine Graham wrote recently, "The extraordinary quality of Herb's eye, his insight and comments immediately stood out. When the *Post* was struggling for its existence, Herb was one of its major assets, as he has been throughout his 50 years here. The *Post* and Herblock are forever intertwined. If the *Post* is his forum, he helped create it. And he has been its shining light."

In Washington, he has achieved a rare freedom from editorial control, sharing preliminary sketches with trusted office colleagues before selecting and creating a final cartoon for publication. He and the *Post* were in agreement on the excesses of the "anticommunist era" and the damage caused by the reckless opportunism of McCarthy. Later, however, during the Vietnam War, he came more and more to oppose the American government's policy, and his cartoons ran counter to the newspaper's editorial position.

A strong believer in civil liberties, he directed cartoons against the House Committee on Un-American Activities from its earliest days under Congressman Dies in the 1930s until its expiration decades later. Whatever the motives of some individual committee members, he held to the view that there was something ironically wrong and not in the American tradition about a group of congressmen setting themselves up to decide who and what they chose to label "Un-American."

Herb Block's "instincts are common-sensical," according to Katharine Graham, Chairman of the Washington Post Company. His steadfast support for established values and reform policies transcend party politics: "My feeling was best expressed in a statement by a Republican President, Abraham Lincoln, that the object of government is to do for people what they need to have done but cannot do at all, or cannot do as well for themselves."

Numerous editors have attempted unsuccessfully over the years to influence or alter his cartoons, suggesting he take a different approach or voice a different opinion. Herb Block has invariably demurred, standing by his work and upholding his now legendary reputation for editorial independence. A thoughtful journalist and gifted cartoonist, he is universally admired for his integrity. Recently Katharine Graham wrote of him, "Herb fought for and earned a unique position at the paper: one of complete independence of anybody and anything."

Herb Block's longevity is due in part to the journalistic passion inspired by his father and older brothers. Unlike many cartoonists, he chooses to work daily in his office adjacent to the newsroom rather than drawing at home or in an isolated studio. He takes full advantage of the instant access proximity provides to expert verification of facts and the latest news from Washington and around the globe. Close attention to breaking news and consultation with coworkers keeps his work fresh and his mind open to viewing new issues.

When a drawing goes to press, however, it is Herb Block's own, without question. Through the decades he has remained true to certain issues and principles: supporting civil rights measures, gun control, campaign finance reform, funding for education and democracy for residents for the District of Columbia, among other issues. "Taking one issue at a time and one administration at a time and dealing with it the way you see it," is how he describes his approach. Raised in what he says might now be called "secular humanism," he takes a dim view of politicians who see religiosity as essential to public service. His longtime assistant, Jean Rickard, suggests that his parents instilled in him a strong sense of wrong and right, the confidence to express his views openly and the courage to stand up for what is right. For example, on the issue of racism, which Herb Block began addressing immediately after World War II (in advance of virtually all other American cartoonists), he notes "I never had those feelings growing up. My father and mother felt that you should simply be a good citizen and think about the other guy."

Herb Block has been thinking about "the other guy" throughout his career.

For more than seventy years, cartoon after cartoon, day after day, he has chronicled the best America has to offer and the worst, from the depths of the Great Depression into a new millennium. No editorial cartoonist in American history, not even Thomas Nast, has made a more lasting impression on the nation than Herbert Block. His influence has been enormous, both on his profession and the general public, although he modestly sloughs off such praise with anecdotes. One was about a comment related to *Post* publisher Phil Graham during the 1954 Army-McCarthy hearings. Walter Winchell told Graham that he had come upon Senator McCarthy shaving at midday and complaining that he had to shave twice a day now on account of that guy [Herb Block] and his cartoons. Apparently his caricatures of the senator as an unshaven, belligerent Neanderthal in a suit found their mark. When asked if he feels he played a role in checking McCarthy's rise to power, Herb Block quietly responds, "I sure tried to." Richard Nixon expressed a similar reaction to the cartoons, saying at one point that he had to "erase the Herblock image."

Humor has been one of his greatest assets, drawing people in, encouraging them to read the cartoons and consider his opinions. Laughter warms the coldest heart and lends perspective to serious issues and events. "I enjoy humor and comedy," he says, "and like to get fun into the work." Humor is an important vehicle for delivering a message, making "it a little easier for the medicine to go down." Herb Block's cartoons may never cure cancer or the common cold, but for the better part of a century they have helped ward off the ill effects of war, bigotry, economic opportunism, political arrogance, and social injustice. What more could we ask of one man?

Harry L. Katz
Head Curator
Prints and Photographs Division

"Light! More light!"—
Goethe's last words
between 1933 and 1939
Ink, crayon, and opaque white over blue
pencil underdrawing on layered paper
Published by NEA Service, Inc. (6)

In his drive to make Germany into a Fascist
Aryan empire, Adolf Hitler took control of
all aspects of religion, art, literature, and
cultural life. Nineteenth-century poet,
novelist, playwright, scientist and thinker
Johann Wolfgang von Goethe, embodied
for many the best of German thought
and culture.

In one of Charles Schulz's *Peanuts* strips, Lucy announces that she's going to be a political cartoonist "lashing out with my crayon." Just as Charlie Brown asks the subject of her work, she strikes the paper with such a bold stroke that it snaps her crayon in half. "I'm lashing out," she says, "at the people who make these stupid crayons."

I don't believe in the Lucy method of deciding first to "lash out" and then picking a convenient target. But as a person with definite opinions, she might have done well to stick with cartooning anyhow.

A wide range of work comes under the heading of editorial or political cartooning today, including gag cartoons on current topics. I enjoy many of these and usually put some fun into my work. But I still feel that the political cartoon should have a view to express, that it should have some purpose beyond the chuckle. So what I'm talking about here is the cartoon as an opinion medium.

The political cartoon is not a news story and not an oil portrait. It's essentially a means for poking fun, for puncturing pomposity.

Cartooning is an irreverent form of expression, and one particularly suited to scoffing at the high and the mighty. If the prime role of a free press is to serve as critic of government, cartooning is often the cutting edge of that criticism.

We seldom do cartoons about public officials that say: "Congratulations on keeping your hands out of the public till," or "It was awfully nice of you to tell the truth yesterday." Public officials are *supposed to* keep their hands out of the till and to tell the truth. With only one shot a day, cartoons are generally drawn about officials we feel are *not* serving the public interest. And we usually support the "good guys" by directing our efforts at their opponents.

For people who think political cartoons are inclined to be negative, a good explanation is in the story of the school teacher who asked the children in her class to give examples of their kindness to birds and animals. One boy told of how he had taken in a kitten on a cold night and fed it. A girl told of how she had found an injured bird and cared for it. When the teacher asked the next boy if he could give an example of his kindness to nature's creatures, he said, "Yes ma'am. One time I kicked a boy for kicking a dog."

In our line of work, we frequently show our love for our fellow men by kicking big boys who kick underdogs. In opposing corruption, suppression of rights and abuse of government office, the political cartoon has always served as a special prod—a reminder to public servants that they ARE public servants.

That is the relationship of the cartoonist to government, and I think the job is best performed by judging officials on their public records and not on the basis of their cozy confidences.

As for the cartoonist's relationship to the rest of the newspaper, that depends on the individual cartoonist and the paper. The editorial page cartoon in the *Washington Post* is a signed expression of personal opinion. In this respect, it is like a column or other signed article—as distinguished from the editorials, which express the policy of the newspaper itself.

Other newspapers operate differently. On some, the cartoon is drawn to accompany an editorial. The cartoonist may sit in on a daily conference, where the content of editorials and cartoons is worked out. Or he may be given copies of the editorials before publication.

A completely different arrangement is followed when the cartoonist simply sends in his work, sometimes from another city. Still other variations include cartoonists submitting sketches (one or several) for editorial approval.

I draw my cartoons at the *Washington Post,* but don't submit sketches or sit in on editorial conferences. And I don't see the editorials in advance. This is for much the same reason that I don't read "idea letters." I like to start from scratch, thinking about what to say, without having to "unthink" other ideas first. That's something like the old business of trying not to think of an elephant for five minutes. It's easier if nobody has mentioned an elephant at all.

In my case, the actual work process is more methodical than inspirational—despite the apparent aimlessness of strolls out of the office, chats with friends, shuffling papers, lining up drawing materials, and other diversions that may or may not have to do with creativity. It's methodical compared to the popular impression that "getting an idea" consists of waiting for a cartoon light bulb to flash on overhead.

The day's work begins with reading the newspapers, usually starting the night before with the first edition of the *Washington Post,* and making notes on possible subjects. I also flip on the radio or TV for late news developments. This practice began when I was just about to turn in a finished cartoon one day, only to learn that a major story had broken and kept the newsroom people too busy to tell me about it. The quick return to the drawing board to produce a new cartoon in minutes was an experience I wouldn't want to repeat. And with broadcast reports on the hour or even the half hour, I now occasionally pass along late-breaking news to others.

Unless there is one subject of overriding importance or timeliness on a particular day, or some special outrage, I generally try to narrow down the list of subjects to two or three. Next comes the business of thinking about what it is that needs to be said—and then getting the comment into graphic form, which involves drawing several rough sketches.

It is hard to say just when a thought turns into a cartoon. In writing or speaking, we all use phrases that lend themselves to visual images. Where you might say that a politician is in trouble up to his neck, a drawing might show him as a plumber in a flooded basement or a boy at the dike with his chin just above the water line. On one occasion when a public figure obviously was not telling the truth, I did a sketch of him speaking, with a tongue that was shaped exactly like a table fork. These are pretty simple examples, but they may provide some clue to how concepts develop into drawings.

It may not sound very exciting or "cartoony," but to me the basic idea is the same as it ought to be with a written opinion—to try to say the right thing. Putting the thought into a picture comes second. Caricature also figures in the cartoons. But the total cartoon is more important than just fun with faces and figures.

I mention this because it is a common conversational gambit to ask cartoonists if they're having a good time with some well-known face. And when media people are doing articles on a new political personality, they often phone cartoonists to ask what it is about the politician's features that grabs them. Some even ask which candidate you would like to see elected on the basis of "drawability." That's like asking a writer what person he wants elected on the basis of whether the candidate's name lends itself to puns.

I have not yet yielded to the temptation to answer such questions by saying I liked Ronald Reagan's right ear lobe or Jimmy Carter's left nostril. Actually, anyone can be caricatured. And if a cartoonist needed a public figure with Dumbo-the-Elephant ears or a Jimmy Durante nose, he'd have to be pretty hard up for ideas *and* drawing.

From time to time the question of cartoon fairness comes up—with some practitioners asserting that they are not supposed to be fair. This is a view I don't share. Caricature itself is sometimes cited as being unfair because it plays on physical characteristics. But like any form of satire, caricature employs exaggeration—clearly recognized as such. Also the portrayal of a person is often part of the opinion. For example, President George Bush was associated with words like "Read my lips" and "The vision thing." Emphasizing his overhanging upper lip and squinty eyes expressed a view identifying him with his words. I think fairness depends on the cartoon— on whether the view is based on actual statements, actions or inactions.

Questions of fairness are not confined to pictures. Some broadcasters and columnists regularly earn championship belts for fighting straw men. (Those "liberals" want the government to take all your money and run your lives in Washington. Those "conservatives" want to see your kids starve to death.) Incidentally I would like to see a better word than "conservative" for some who are not eager to conserve basic rights or the environment.

A columnist who opposes political campaign funding reform—based on his interpretation of the First Amendment—wrote a piece in which he pointed out that we spend more on potato chips than on political campaigns. But, if true, the purchase and consumption of potato chips, whatever they do to our diets, can hardly be compared to the purchase and corruption of public offices. I'd guess the columnist who reached for that statistical irrelevance probably regards cartoons for campaign funding reform as "gross caricatures."

But back to the drawing board and the sketches—

A series of "roughs" may approach a subject from different angles or may be variations on a theme. This is where other people come into the picture—or, more accurately, where I bring the pictures to other people. By showing sketches to a few colleagues on the paper, I often find out which sketch expresses a thought most clearly. The purpose of these trial runs is not only to get individual reactions but also to get out any bugs that might be in the cartoon ideas.

One of the advantages of working at the *Washington Post* is the access to information about government and assorted news items. Reporters, researchers and other staff members are available—with special knowledge about subjects they have dealt with. They also know where to find answers to questions about who said what or exactly what happened when. And computers now make it possible to recall statements and records of all kinds.

A sketch on arms programs or military costs, for example, is one I'd particularly want to discuss with the Pentagon correspondent. A writer covering the courts can tell me if I've missed anything in a decision. Capitol Hill writers, familiar with the exact status of congressional bills, can tell if a sketch on a piece of legislation is well-timed. Staff members may also have information that helps me decide which cartoon is the best bet for that day. Such help—not "ideas for cartoons," but background information and relevant facts—is of enormous value.

I'm a deadline pusher, and one reason the finished cartoon is usually a last-gasp down-to-the-wire effort is because of the time spent on sketches. I work on them as long as possible. And after deciding on one, I send a Xerox copy of it to the editor's office.

Other cartoonists—as well as other papers—prefer different arrangements. One cartoonist told me he had tried for years to get the kind of freedom I have on the *Post*. When he finally got it, he found the decision-making to be a burden. He went back to asking an editor to make the daily choice.

I enjoy the freedom to express my own ideas in my own way. And this is also consistent with the *Washington Post* policy expressed by the late publisher, Eugene Meyer, who said he believed in getting people who knew what they were doing and then letting them do it.

One of the things that has made the *Washington Post* great is the fact that it *does* provide for differing views instead of offering a set of written and drawn opinions all bearing the stamp of a single person.

Over the years, there have been differences between the cartoons and the editorials on issues, on emphasis and on performances of individual public figures.

In 1952, for example, the *Washington Post* endorsed General Dwight Eisenhower for president before either major party had made nominations. The cartoons expressed my unhappiness with the campaign conducted by Eisenhower and his choice for vice president, Richard Nixon—and expressed my clear preference for candidate Adlai Stevenson.

About 1965, with a different editor and a different publisher, the cartoons focused more and more on President Johnson's "credibility gap" and his escalation of the war in Vietnam, while the editorials generally supported the president and his Vietnam policy. Even on this extremely divisive issue, the editor and I respected each other's views.

Later, the cartoons and editorials diverged on other subjects. For example, in the 1970s I did a series of cartoons opposing the confirmation of Clement Haynsworth to the Supreme Court—a view not shared in the editorials. But we were in agreement in opposing the next nominee— G. Harold Carswell.

During the Clinton administration, I did not share in the *Post's* approval of the expansion of the North American Treaty Organization (NATO) after the collapse of the Soviet Union. And the cartoons hardly matched the editorials on Independent Counsel Kenneth Starr—which acknowledged that he had made mistakes in the probe of President Clinton's relationships but saw him as a victim of a vicious organized attack.

On important issues involving civil rights and civil liberties the editorials and cartoons have been in general agreement. There was no possible doubt about the stands they shared on the attempted censorship involved in the publication of the Pentagon Papers on Vietnam or the culmination of the Nixon scandals in Watergate. And they have both been involved in the long continuous battles for campaign finance reform and gun controls and tobacco industry curbs.

But even where the general viewpoints have been the same, there have been times when I knew a publisher or editor would have preferred my using a different approach. During the Watergate disclosures, I did a "naked Nixon." This might have seemed like *lèse majesté* to an editor but was *au naturel* for a cartoonist.

I've often summed up the role of the cartoonist as that of the boy in the Hans Christian Andersen story who says the emperor has no clothes on. And that seemed to be just what was called for during this phase of the "imperial presidency."

What a written piece can do more easily than a cartoon is to comment on a subject that requires giving background information. Wordiness can be awkward in a cartoon—though sometimes needed to explain an issue or provide dialogue. But a cartoon at times can say something that might be harder to put into words. The one of Nixon hanging between the tapes comments not only on his situation at the time, but on his veracity and honesty—without using any words other than his own.

As for a comparison of words and pictures—each has its role. Each is capable of saying something necessary or something irrelevant—of reaching a right conclusion or a wrong one.

A cartoon does not tell everything about a subject. It's not supposed to. No written piece tells everything either. As far as words are concerned, there is no safety in numbers. The test of a written or drawn commentary is whether it gets at an essential truth.

As for subject matter, I don't believe there should be any sacred cows. But there's no obligation for the cartoonist to deal with a topic unless he feels there is a point that needs to be made. Regardless of Lucy's view, the object is not to "lash out" just because the means is at hand.

There is no shortage of subjects for opinions. I don't long for public misfortunes or official crooks to provide "material for cartoons." Hard as it may be for some people to believe—I don't miss malefactors when they are gone from public life. There are more things amiss than you can shake a crayon at.

If the time should come when political figures and all the rest of us sprout angel wings, there will still be different views on the proper whiteness and fluffiness of the wings, as well as flaps over their flapping, speed, and altitude. And there will still be something funny about a halo that's worn slightly askew.

When that happy heaven-on-earth day comes, I'd still like to be drawing cartoons. I wouldn't want to see any head angel throwing his weight around.

Herbert Block

THE PORTFOLIO

"It's okay—We're hunting Communists"
October 31, 1947
Ink, graphite, and opaque white over graphite
underdrawing on layered paper
Published in the *Washington Post* (18)

The Cold War revived the anticommunist hysteria
that had gripped the United States after World
War I. In 1947 Congress revived the House
Committee on Un-American Activities (HUAC)—
opposed by Herb Block since its inception in
the 1930's—and declared by President Truman
to be itself the most un-American activity.

Herb Block comments: *"Chaired by
J. Parnell Thomas (later convicted and jailed
for accepting kickbacks) HUAC investigated
suspected Communist Party infiltration into the
federal government, labor unions and especially
Hollywood, where it shared klieg lights with
movie celebrities. The FBI, under J. Edgar
Hoover, helped provide the committee with
material from its aptly named "raw files." Some
producers, directors and screen writers refused
to testify or to play the "name game"—in which
the committee demanded the names of
associates, who could then be called on to
name others—thus providing an ever-expanding
list of suspects to be summoned. Among those
who successfully stood up to the committee were
playwright Arthur Miller and actress Judy
Holliday. But countless others were blacklisted
and their careers ruined. All this was done in
the name of patriotism."*

"IT'S OKAY --- WE'RE HUNTING COMMUNISTS"

ROOM WITH A VIEW

HERBLOCK
©1949 THE WASHINGTON POST CO.

SENATE DEBATES HOUSING, SLUM CLEARANCE

Room with a view
April 22, 1949
Ink, graphite, and opaque white over graphite underdrawing on layered paper
Published in the *Washington Post* (23)

Despite efforts to clear slums and replace them with low-cost public housing, inequities continued to exist in America's cities. Herb Block adds: *"The contrasts are particularly noticeable in the nation's capital, where a well-housed Congress dominates attempts at self-rule."*

Tick-tock, tick-tock

January 11, 1949
Ink, graphite, and opaque white over
graphite underdrawing on layered paper
Published in the *Washington Post* (20)

Herb Block's "Mr. Atom" personification of
"the bomb" in many cartoons has reminded
readers of the threat of nuclear annihilation.
Here, a new international "atomic clock"—
developed by using atomic waves to provide
a world standard of measurement—gives its
own reminder, as the great powers fail to
reach agreement on the control of atomic
energy.

"TICK-TOCK TICK-TOCK"

"HOW MUCH DO YOU FIGURE THIS ONE WOULD COST?"

HERBLOCK
©1950 THE WASHINGTON POST CO.

"What do you figure this one would cost?"
September 12, 1950
Ink, graphite, and opaque white over graphite underdrawing on layered paper
Published in the *Washington Post* (29)

Pressure for campaign finance reform is not new. Herb Block has been pointing out for five decades how special interests use campaign donations to gain influence. In 1950 Congress failed to take action on a proposal by a House committee to set up an inquiry into the relationship between lobbying and election campaigns. The issue—and the cartoon—are fresh today.

"I have here in my hand . . ."
May 7, 1954
Ink, graphite, opaque white, and
overlay over graphite underdrawing
on layered paper
Published in the *Washington Post* (34)

In 1954, Senator Joseph McCarthy
overreached himself when he took on
the United States Army, accusing it of
promoting communists. The Senate held
special hearings, known as the Army-
McCarthy hearings, which were among the
first to be televised nationally. In the course
of testimony, McCarthy submitted evidence
that was identified as fraudulent. As both
public and politicians watched the bullying
antics of the senator, they became
increasingly disenchanted. Before the year
was out, McCarthy, whose charges had first
hit the headlines in February 1950, was
censured by his colleagues for "conduct
unbecoming a senator."

HERBLOCK
©1959 THE WASHINGTON POST CO.

Poplarville, Mississippi, U. S. A., 1959
April 28, 1959
Ink, graphite, and opaque white over graphite underdrawing on layered paper
Published in the *Washington Post* (43)

Although in the 1950s some progress was made toward attaining civil rights for African Americans, lynchings continued until the late 1960s. On April 25, 1959, a group abducted Charles Parker from prison in Poplarville, Mississippi, where he awaited trial on charges of raping a white woman. On May 4, the FBI found his body in the Pearl River near Bogalusha, Louisiana, executed with two bullets.

**"Mirror, mirror, on the wall,
who's the fairest one of all?"**
January 2, 1960
Ink, graphite, and opaque white over
graphite underdrawing on layered paper
Published in the *Washington Post* (44)

In this cartoon from the beginning of 1960,
Herb Block shows Vice-President Richard
Nixon preparing to run for the presidential
nomination that year—depicting him on the
basis of his past record as the witch-like
character from Snow White. Nixon won the
Republican nomination and lost to Senator
John F. Kennedy that fall.

"All are gone, the old familiar fasces"
July 5, 1962
Ink, graphite, and opaque white over
graphite underdrawing on layered paper
Published in the *Washington Post* (50)

By 1962, Hitler, Mussolini and many other
military dictators of the first part of the
twentieth century had been driven from
power. Still grasping the reins was their
ally, General Francisco Franco, whose
Fascist government ruled Spain. In the title,
Herb Block modifies a Charles Lamb line,
replacing "faces" with "fasces," the word
for an ax tied into a bundle of rods that
was the ancient Roman symbol for authority
and later the source for the term "fascism."

"HOW ABOUT ONE MORE TRY?"

"How about one more try?"
May 29, 1963
Ink, graphite, and opaque white over
graphite underdrawing on layered paper
Published in the *Washington Post* (52)

In spring 1962, President Kennedy, Prime
Minister Harold Macmillan of Britain, and
Nikita Khrushchev of the Soviet Union were
wrestling with a formula for a nuclear test
agreement. Kennedy told a press conference
that if an accord were not reached soon,
"the genie [might be] out of the bottle." On
May 29, the *Washington Post* reported that
thirty-four senators, led by Senator Hubert
Humphrey and Senator Thomas J. Dodd,
had proposed a ban on atmospheric and
underwater testing. A limited Test Ban
Treaty was finally ratified in September
1963, the first limitation on the production
of nuclear weapons.

The other ascent into the unknown
June 10, 1965
Ink, graphite, and opaque white over
graphite underdrawing on layered paper
Published in the *Washington Post* (61)

During the presidential campaign of 1964,
President Lyndon Johnson suggested that
Republican candidate Barry Goldwater
could not be trusted to keep the U.S out of
war. But not long after his election, Johnson
had increased American involvement in the
Vietnam War and moved ultimately to take
over the war itself. In the same week that
NASA sent the Gemini 4 space capsule into
orbit, setting new records for a two-man
flight, the State Department announced that
Johnson had authorized a potential role
for direct American military involvement
in Vietnam if requested by the South
Vietnamese authorities. Herb Block was
prescient in his view that this constituted
a major step in the involvement of U.S.
forces in Indochina.

.

Fiddler

July 25, 1967

Ink, graphite, and opaque white over graphite underdrawing on layered paper Copyright 1967, Herblock, *The Washington Post*, distributed by Hall Syndicate, Inc. (65)

In 1967, President Johnson hailed the "good life" in the United States, as living conditions for Americans reached high levels. However, inner city residents, especially blacks experiencing poverty and racial injustice, felt no share in it. During the summer of 1967, riots broke out in several American cities. Some black leaders urged crowds to resist police in Atlanta in June. Protests against police brutality and unemployment spread to Buffalo, Newark, Detroit, and many other cities across the United States. In response, on July 19 the House passed a bill that made it a federal crime to cross state lines to incite a riot.

Herb Block comments: *"On a two-track presidency, the same Lyndon Johnson who expanded the war and kept increasing the casualties abroad benefitted from the Congress he brought in with him in his 1964 landslide to increase domestic reforms. He put through Medicare, stepped-up aid to education, and a new housing law; created the Department of Transportation and the Department of Urban Development; and put through the 1965 voting rights law and the Civil Rights Act of 1968."*

"She might have invaded Russia"
September 3, 1968
Ink, graphite, and opaque white over
graphite underdrawing on layered paper
Published in the *Washington Post* (68)

In January 1968, moderate communists
came to power in Czechoslovakia,
inaugurating a period of increasing
democratization known as the "Prague
Spring." The Soviet Union became
increasingly concerned that the Czech
experiment might spread to other countries
in the Soviet Bloc. During the night of
August 20–21, Soviet troops, joined by
the forces of satellite countries, occupied
the country by force.

National-security blanket
May 27, 1973
Ink, graphite, and opaque white over
graphite underdrawing on layered paper
Published in the *Washington Post* (75)

On May 22, 1973, President Richard Nixon
admitted that he had concealed aspects of
the case involving the break-in at
Democratic headquarters in the Watergate.
He did so, he said, to protect national
security "operations." Nixon affirmed his
innocence and said he would stay in office.
Herb Block, whose earliest cartoons critical
of Nixon had appeared twenty-five years
before, saw Nixon seeking cover amidst
evidence of wiretapping, break-in, political
sabotage, laundered FBI funds from Mexico
and other illegal activities.

[Nixon awash in his office]
June 26, 1973
Ink, graphite, and opaque white over
graphite underdrawing on paper
Published in the *Washington Post* (76)

By June 1973, the country had become
transfixed by the investigation of Watergate
via the televised hearings of the Senate
Select Committee on Presidential Campaign
Activities. On June 25, former presidential
counsel John Dean began his testimony,
the first before the committee to directly
accuse President Nixon of involvement in
the coverup.

"Read me what it says, Dad"
June 8, 1977
Ink, crayon, and opaque white over blue
pencil underdrawing on paper
Published in the *Washington Post* (84)

In *Herblock on All Fronts,* the cartoonist
wrote: "Depreciation in dollars, in products,
and in entertainment has also extended to
education. Here it is not a case of the fast
buck but of the fast bucking-the-kid-along-
to-the-next-grade. It produces graduates
who can hardly make their way through
a phone book or figure the cost of four
twenty-five-cent items in a grocery store."

"AH, INDEPENDENCE DAY — THE GLORIOUS FOURTH! DO SEE THAT THE NATIVES GET A NICE FIREWORKS DISPLAY"

SENATE

END TAXATION-WITHOUT-REPRESENTATION IN THE DISTRICT OF COLUMBIA

U.S. SENATORS: BRING DEMOCRACY TO THE NATION'S CAPITAL

©1978 HERBLOCK

**"Ah, Independence Day—
The glorious Fourth! Do see
that the natives get a nice
fireworks display"**
June 30, 1978
Ink, graphite, crayon, porous point pen,
opaque white, and overlays over blue
pencil underdrawing on paper
Published in the *Washington Post* (89)

As a resident of Washington, D.C., since 1946, Herb Block has actively promoted democracy for the half million or so residents of the District of Columbia. In 1978, with backing from President Carter's administration, a constitutional amendment to provide the District with representation in the Senate and the House was approved by the required two-thirds majority in Congress, but lobbyists stopped it before it could gain ratification by the required number of states.

Herb Block comments: *"The residents of the District of Columbia pay the Federal income tax. They also pay District income tax that is higher than that in nearly every state. District residents already pay federal and local taxes on sales and property and are required to fulfill the same calls to duty—including military service—as other Americans. But they have no voting representation on the floor of either house of Congress. Additionally, the District's limited home rule is subject to strict congressional control. This control is so complete that in 1998, Congress even prevented the counting of ballots cast on a D.C. local referendum."*

Invasion of the corporate
body snatchers
April 21, 1985
Ink, crayon, porous point pen, opaque
white, and overlay over blue pencil
underdrawing on paper
Published in the *Washington Post* (97)

In this cartoon, Herb Block anticipated the
super-giant super-mergers that came later.
In the 1980s, the deregulation of banking
in the United States allowed financiers to
use unprecedented and risky tactics.
Financial innovations such as junk bonds
encouraged corporate mergers, leveraged
buyouts, and hostile takeovers at a
phenomenal rate. By April 1985, the failure
of many savings and loan institutions, even
including a bail-out involving one of
President Bush's sons, Neil, cost U.S.
taxpayers hundreds of billions of dollars.
It was described by former Attorney
General Dick Thornburgh as the biggest
white collar scandal in history. Herb Block
says, *"It was swept under a very large rug."*

Arms payoff for hostage release
November 11, 1986
Ink, crayon, porous point pen, opaque
white, tonal film overlay, and overlay over
blue pencil underdrawing on paper
Published in the *Washington Post* (99)

On November 2, 1986, an American
hostage was released by an Iranian group
that had held him captive for more than
seventeen months. It was soon reported
that his release was linked to a transfer of
military spare parts to Iran. Reagan said,
"the commenting on a story that came out
of the Middle East and that, to us, has no
foundation—all of that is making it more
difficult to get the other hostages out."

Herb Block comments: *"But 'the story
that came out of the Middle East' was true,
and the trading of arms actually provided
an incentive for the taking of more
hostages. The Iran-Contra scandals were
triple-decked. They involved (1) the trading
of arms for hostages, (2) the selling of arms
to Iran, an embargoed nation, and (3) the
diversion of funds to aid the rebel
Nicaraguan contras—a violation of an act
of Congress. Appearing on television,
Reagan said forcefully, 'We did not—repeat
not—trade weapons or anything else for
hostages.' When this was proven to be
untrue, he later made a carefully worded
retraction. He left it to his Attorney General
Meese to disclose the diversion of arms-
sales funds to aid the contras."*

"People's Republic"
June 6, 1989
Ink, crayon, porous point pen,
and opaque white, over blue pencil
underdrawing on paper
Published in the *Washington Post* (105)

On June 3–4, 1989, Chinese army troops
and tanks rolled into the Tiananmen Square
area in Beijing to crush student-led pro-
democracy protests that had begun in mid-
April. Residents of other cities in China and
nations worldwide protested the bloody
crackdown. Casualties were estimated at
5,000. Herb Block reprinted this cartoon ten
years later as a reminder of the Chinese
rulers that Americans were dealing with.

"PEOPLE'S REPUBLIC"

THE SORCERER'S APPRENTICE

BUDGET COOKERY

VOODOO ECONOMICS

©1990 HERBLOCK

The sorcerer's apprentice
October 7, 1990
Ink, crayon, porous point pen, opaque
white, and overlay over blue pencil
underdrawing on paper
Published in the *Washington Post* (106)

George Bush ran against Ronald Reagan
for the Republican nomination during the
1980 presidential campaign, criticizing his
opponent's economic program as "voodoo
economics." Herb Block comments: *"Later,
on being considered for the vice-presidency,
he not only switched to supporting Reagan's
economic policies but did 180-degree turns
to change from a Planned Parenthood
supporter to a "right-to-lifer" and a sudden
convert to all of Reagan's social policies,
including teaching of "creationism" with
evolution, and a constitutional amendment
to bring organized vocal prayer into the
public schools. He was also for a
constitutional amendment to require a
balanced budget. He got the job. And four
years later The Big Job. But his 1988
pledge, 'Read my lips. No new taxes'—
came back to bite him when he agreed
to a budget plan to increase taxes."*

Balance
February 4, 1998
Ink, crayon, porous point pen, opaque
white, and overlays over blue pencil
underdrawing on paper
Published in the *Washington Post* (114)

Allegations of an affair between President
Bill Clinton and former White House intern
Monica Lewinsky became public on January
21, 1998. Although Clinton repeatedly and
forcefully denied any improper relationship,
later testimony proved his statements untrue
and resulted in a House vote of impeachment.
While fending off these accusations, Clinton
proposed the first balanced federal budget in
nearly thirty years.

SPEAKERS ON BEHALF OF THE KOSOVO MASSACRED AND HOMELESS

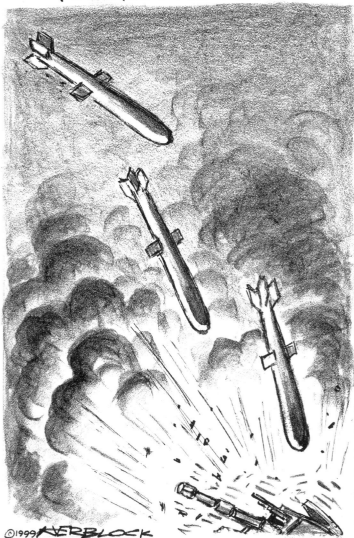

©1999 HERBLOCK

***Speakers on behalf of the Kosovo
massacred and homeless***
March 25, 1999
Ink, crayon, porous point pen, opaque
white, and overlays over blue pencil underdrawing on paper
Published in the Washington Post (137)

On March 23, 1999, NATO and the
United States ordered air strikes against the
Yugoslav military after Serbian President
Slobodan Milosevic refused to halt his
campaign against Kosovo Albanians. The
air attacks began on the night of March 24,
hitting Yugoslav targets, including the
capitol city of Belgrade. President Clinton
evoked images of Nazi atrocities during
World War II to lend moral weight to the
decision to attack Yugoslavia. The American
people, in general, responded favorably
to NATO's action

"Kids these days! Craziness in schools movies, video games— terrible! Here—Try this dandy!"
April 28, 1999
Ink, crayon, porous point pen, opaque white, and overlays over blue pencil underdrawing on paper
Published in the *Washington Post* (118)

This cartoon appeared shortly after the Columbine High School massacre in Littleton, Colorado, in which two teenagers shot and killed twelve of their fellow students and a teacher before turning their weapons on themselves. This horrifying event followed other widely reported acts of violence with firearms in U.S. schools. Many joined the gun lobby in seeking causes everywhere except in the easy availability of firearms.

"SAID ALICE...'IT'S THE STUPIDEST TEA-PARTY I EVER WAS AT IN ALL MY LIFE'"

©1999 HERBLOCK

"Said Alice . . . 'It's the stupidest tea-party I ever was at in all my life"
October 31, 1999
Ink, crayon, porous point pen, opaque white, and overlays over blue pencil underdrawing on paper
Published in the *Washington Post* (120)

On October 25, 1999, presidential candidate Patrick Buchanan switched from the Republican Party to the Reform Party, creating divisiveness within the emerging third party because his political platform differed markedly from that of founder Ross Perot. In the meantime, real estate magnate Donald Trump had formally filed paperwork establishing his Reform Party candidacy on October 24, 1999. Trump was favored as the "Stop Buchanan" candidate, but several months later, in February 2000, he withdrew from the race. On August 11, 2000, Patrick Buchanan accepted the presidential nomination from one wing of a decidedly split Reform Party. For Herb Block, the situation evoked one of Sir John Tenniel's famous illustrations for Lewis Carroll's *Alice's Adventures in Wonderland.*

It's still a representative form of government—they represent us"

May 18, 2000

Ink, crayon, porous point pen, opaque white, and overlays over blue pencil underdrawing on paper

Copyright, 2000, Herblock, distributed by Creators Syndicate, Inc. (138)

The unlimited "soft money" raised by national party organizations can be spent on advertisements that skirt the campaign finance reforms brought on by the excess of the Watergate era. Herb Block has consistently pointed out that the skyrocketing campaign contributions and expenditures threaten "government by the people and for the people." As for "free speech" arguments, he notes that there is nothing free about sales of public office to high bidders, who buy and pay for elections and influence.

"IT'S STILL A REPRESENTATIVE FORM OF GOVERNMENT—THEY REPRESENT US"

© 2000 HERBLOCK

HARE AND TORTOISE 2000

©2000 HERBLOCK

Hare and Tortoise 2000
June 18, 2000
Ink, crayon, porous point pen, opaque white, and overlays over blue pencil underdrawing on paper
Copyright, 2000, Herblock, distributed by Creators Syndicate, Inc. (139)

Aesop's fable about the tortoise and the hare became a metaphor for the 2000 pre-convention presidential campaign. Although faster, Al Gore, the hare, seemed to bounce around, while George W. Bush, the tortoise, wheeled steadily ahead. A Bush lead in the polls dropped after Gore's appearance at the mid-summer Democratic convention.

EXHIBITION CHECKLIST

Herblock's Presidents

Well everything helps, 1930 or 1931
Ink over graphite underdrawing with
scratching out on layered paper
Published in the *Chicago Daily News* (3)
LC-USZ62-127207

"O, death! O, change! O, time!" 1937
Ink, crayon, and opaque white over graphite
underdrawing on layered paper
Published by NEA Service, Inc. (8)
LC-USZ62-127205

*"Cannon to right of them, cannon to
left of them,"* February 23, 1948
Ink, graphite, and opaque white over
graphite underdrawing on layered paper
Published in the *Washington Post* (19)
LC-USZ62-127199

*"Tsk Tsk—Somebody Should Do Something
About That,"* April 3, 1956
Reproduction of original drawing
Published in the *Washington Post* (145)

*"Throw him some more flowers honey—let's see
how long he'll keep playing,"* July 18, 1962
Ink, graphite, and opaque white over graphite
underdrawing on layered paper
Published in the *Washington Post* (147)
LC-USZ62-127085

"Ev tu?" June 10, 1966
Ink, graphite, and opaque white over
graphite underdrawing on layered paper
Published in the *Washington Post* (63)
LC-USZ62-127072

National-security blanket, May 27, 1973
Ink, graphite, and opaque white over
graphite underdrawing on layered paper
Published in the *Washington Post* (75)
LC-USZ62-126917

"Gee! A medal from Gen. Goldwater,"
July 2, 1976
Ink, graphite, and opaque white over
graphite underdrawing on paper
Published in the *Washington Post* (82)
LC-USZ62-126887

"It comes out fuzzy," May 21, 1978
Ink, graphite, crayon, porous point pen,
opaque white, and overlays over graphite
underdrawing on paper
Published in the *Washington Post* (88)
LC-USZ62-126935

[Cardboard Ronald Reagan], March 5, 1987
Ink, crayon, porous point pen, and opaque
white, over blue pencil underdrawing on paper
Published in the *Washington Post* (102)
LC-USZ62-126874

I was out of the loop, October 4, 1992
Ink, crayon, porous point pen, and opaque
white, over blue pencil underdrawing on paper
Published in the *Washington Post* (108)
LC-USZ62-126895

Balance, February 4, 1998
Ink, crayon, porous point pen, opaque white, and
overlays over blue pencil underdrawing on paper
Published in the *Washington Post* (114)
LC-USZ62-126900

"Light! More Light!"

"This is the forest primeval—," April 24, 1929
Reproduction of original drawing
Published in the *Chicago Daily News* (1)

The philanthropist, December 5, 1930
Ink and blue pencil over graphite
underdrawing on layered paper
Published in the *Chicago Daily News* (2)
LC-USZ62-127206

Little Goldilocks Riding Hood, between 1930
and 1939
Ink, crayon, and opaque white over blue
pencil underdrawing on layered paper
Published by NEA Service, Inc. (5)
LC-USZ62-127201

"Light! More light!"—Goethe's last words,
between 1933 and 1939
Ink, crayon, and opaque white over blue
pencil underdrawing on layered paper
Published by NEA Service, Inc. (6)
LC-USZ62-127330

"No foreign entanglements," 1935
Ink, crayon, and opaque white over blue
pencil underdrawing on laid paper
Published by NEA Service, Inc. (7)
LC-USZ62-127328

Isn't this what we really want? 1939
Ink, crayon, and opaque white over blue
pencil underdrawing on layered paper
Published by NEA Service, Inc. (4)
LC-USZ62-127208

Losses, 1939
Ink, crayon, and opaque white over
graphite underdrawing on layered paper
Published by NEA Service, Inc. (9)
LC-USZ62-127198

Sending Forth Another Dove

Story of the last seven years, May 1940
Ink, crayon, and opaque white over blue
pencil underdrawing on layered paper
Published by NEA Service, Inc. (11)
LC-USZ62-127213

*Herblock's own history of the year—
The worlds of 1940,* 1940
Ink over graphite underdrawing with
scraping out on layered paper
Published by NEA Service, Inc. (12a-b)
LC-USZ62-127211 (a)
LC-USZ62-127197 (b)

Travelogue, June 1940
Reproduction of original drawing
Published by NEA Service, Inc. (154)

Working on him, 1940 or 1941
Ink, crayon, and opaque white over
graphite underdrawing on layered paper
Published by NEA Service (13)
LC-USZ62-127210

Mr. Stalin revolutionizes the drama,
between 1940 and 1950
Ink, crayon, and opaque white over blue
pencil underdrawing on layered paper
Published by NEA Service, Inc. (10)
LC-USZ62-127209

"Faster!" April 17, 1941
Ink, crayon, and opaque white over
graphite underdrawing on layered paper
Published by NEA Service, Inc. (14)
LC-USZ62-127212

"Fifty-Fifty again, Joe?" May 2, 1941
Ink, crayon, and opaque white over
graphite underdrawing with scraping
out on layered paper
Published by NEA Service, Inc. (15)
LC-USZ62-127203

Sending forth another dove, May 13, 1941
Reproduction of original cartoon drawing.
Published by NEA Service, Inc. (16)

Mussolini, 1941
Ink, crayon, and opaque white over
graphite underdrawing on layered paper
Published by NEA Service, Inc. (17)
LC-USZ62-127200

Tick-Tock Tick-Tock

Tick-tock, tick-tock, January 11, 1949
Ink, graphite, and opaque white over
graphite underdrawing on layered paper
Published in the *Washington Post* (20)
LC-USZ62-127333

*"It's the same thing without mechanical
problems,"* January 26, 1949
Ink, graphite, and opaque white over graphite
underdrawing on layered paper
Published in the *Washington Post* (21)
LC-USZ62-127331

*"We've been using more of a roundish
one,"* May 7, 1951
Ink, graphite, and opaque white over
graphite underdrawing on layered paper
Published in the *Washington Post* (30)
LC-USZ62-126907

Albert Einstein lived here, April 19, 1955
Ink, graphite, and opaque white over
graphite underdrawing on layered paper
Published in the *Washington Post* (37)
LC-USZ62-126902

*"However, we've been pretty successful in
keeping American newspapermen out of
China,"* January 6, 1957
Ink, graphite, and opaque white over
graphite underdrawing on layered paper
Published in the *Washington Post* (41)
LC-USZ62-126903

"All are gone, the old familiar fasces,"
July 5, 1962
Ink, graphite, and opaque white over
graphite underdrawing on layered paper
Published in the *Washington Post* (50)
LC-USZ62-127083

"How about one more try?" May 29, 1963
Ink, graphite, and opaque white over
graphite underdrawing on layered paper
Published in the *Washington Post* (52)
LC-USZ62-127089

Mushrooming cloud, April 1, 1965
Ink, graphite, and opaque white over
graphite underdrawing on layered paper
Published in the *Washington Post* (59)
LC-USZ62-127077

"Fire!"

"It's okay—We're hunting Communists,"
October 31, 1947
Ink, graphite, and opaque white over
graphite underdrawing on layered paper
Published in the *Washington Post* (18)
LC-USZ62-127327

"You read books, eh?" April 24, 1949
Ink, graphite, and opaque white over
graphite underdrawing on layered paper
Published in the *Washington Post* (24)
LC-USZ62-127202

"Fire!" June 17, 1949
Reproduction of original drawing
Published in the *Washington Post* (25)

"You mean I'm supposed to stand on that?" March 29, 1950
Reproduction of original drawing
Published in the *Washington Post* (27)

"We now have new and important evidence," May 8, 1950
Ink, graphite, and opaque white over graphite underdrawing on layered paper
Published in the *Washington Post* (28)
LC-USZ62-126908

"Say, what ever happened to 'freedom-from-fear'?" August 13, 1951
Reproduction of original drawing
Published in the *Washington Post* (31)

Nothing exceeds like excess,
September 12, 1952
Ink, graphite, and opaque white over graphite underdrawing on layered paper
Published in the *Washington Post* (32)
LC-USZ62-126909

"Have a care, sir," March 4, 1954
Reproduction of original drawing
Published in the *Washington Post* (33)

"I have here in my hand . . . ,"
May 7, 1954
Ink, graphite, opaque white, and overlay over graphite underdrawing on layered paper
Published in the *Washington Post* (34)
LC-USZ62-126910

"Stand fast, men—They're armed with marshmallows," August 11, 1954
Reproduction of original drawing
Published in the *Washington Post* (35)

"Here he comes now," October 29, 1954
Reproduction of original drawing
Published in the *Washington Post* (36)

"On this order for a new typewriter ribbon—did you know you forgot to stamp it 'Secret'?" July 25, 1956
Ink, graphite, and opaque white over graphite underdrawing on layered paper
Published in the *Washington Post* (40)
LC-USZ62-127332

Fruits of Victory

Fruits of victory, March 16, 1949
Ink, graphite, and opaque white over graphite underdrawing on layered paper
Published in the *Washington Post* (22)
LC-USZ62-127332

Room with a view, April 22, 1949
Ink, graphite, and opaque white over graphite underdrawing on layered paper
Published in the *Washington Post* (23)
LC-USZ62-127329

"Think this crop is worth saving?"
September 22, 1949
Ink, graphite, and opaque white over graphite underdrawing on layered paper
Published in the *Washington Post* (26)
LC-USZ62-127204

"What do you figure this one would cost?" September 12, 1950
Ink, graphite, and opaque white over graphite underdrawing on layered paper
Published in the *Washington Post* (29)
LC-USZ62-126904

"Be sure to give mine special attention,"
November 23, 1955
Reproduction of original drawing
Published in the *Washington Post* (38)

"Tote dat barge! Lift dat boycott! Ride dat bus!" March 25, 1956
Ink, graphite, and opaque white over graphite underdrawing on layered paper
Published in the *Washington Post* (39)
LC-USZ62-126901

Poplarville, Mississippi, U. S. A., 1959,
April 28, 1959
Ink, graphite, and opaque white over graphite underdrawing on layered paper
Published in the *Washington Post* (43)
LC-USZ62-126905

Split-level living, March 9, 1960
Ink, graphite, and opaque white over graphite underdrawing on layered paper
Published in the *Washington Post* (45)
LC-USZ62-127080

"Pray keep moving, brother,"
August 14, 1960
Ink, graphite, and opaque white over graphite underdrawing on layered paper
Published in the *Washington Post* (46)
LC-USZ62-127075

Animal Farm

"Mirror, mirror, on the wall, who's the fairest one of all?" January 2, 1960
Ink, graphite, and opaque white over graphite underdrawing on layered paper
Published in the *Washington Post* (44)
LC-USZ62-127079

Animal farm, April 2, 1961
Ink, graphite, and opaque white over graphite underdrawing on layered paper
Published in the *Washington Post* (47)
LC-USZ62-127074

"It's all right to seat them. They're not Americans," April 27, 1961
Ink, graphite, and opaque white over graphite underdrawing on layered paper
Published in the *Washington Post* (48)
LC-USZ62-127069

"I help to support the establishments I have mentioned; they cost enough, and those who are badly off must go there." —A Christmas Carol, November 29, 1961
Ink, graphite, and opaque white over graphite underdrawing on layered paper
Published in the *Washington Post* (49)
LC-USZ62-127070

"What do they expect us to do—listen to the kids pray at home?" June 18, 1963
Ink, graphite, and opaque white over graphite underdrawing on layered paper
Published in the *Washington Post* (53)
LC-USZ62-127087

*"Sorry, but you have an incurable
skin condition,"* July 4, 1963
Ink, graphite, and opaque white over
graphite underdrawing on layered paper
Published in the *Washington Post* (54)
LC-USZ62-127084

*"And remember, nothing can be accomplished
by taking to the streets,"* September 6, 1963
Ink, graphite, and opaque white over
graphite underdrawing on layered paper
Published in the *Washington Post* (55)
LC-USZ62-127088

"Kindly move over a little, gentlemen,"
January 26, 1965
Ink, graphite, and opaque white over
graphite underdrawing on layered paper
Published in the *Washington Post* (56)
LC-USZ62-127078

*"I got one of 'em just as she almost made
it back to the church,"* March 9, 1965
Ink, graphite, and opaque white over
graphite underdrawing on layered paper
Published in the *Washington Post* (57)
LC-USZ62-127073

Jericho, U. S. A., March 21, 1965
Ink, graphite, and opaque white over
graphite underdrawing on layered paper
Published in the *Washington Post* (58)
LC-USZ62-127076

The Other Ascent Into the Unknown

*"It's like the gun lobby guys say—Laws
interfere wit' us sportsmen,"* June 6, 1965
Ink, graphite, and opaque white over
graphite underdrawing on layered paper
Published in the *Washington Post* (60)
LC-USZ62-127092

The other ascent into the unknown,
June 10, 1965
Ink, graphite, and opaque white over
graphite underdrawing on layered paper
Published in the *Washington Post* (61)
LC-USZ62-127068

"Our position hasn't changed at all,"
June 17, 1965
Ink, graphite, and opaque white over
graphite underdrawing on layered paper
Published in the *Washington Post* (62)
LC-USZ62-127071

*"It says here Congress is anxious to get
out of town,"* October 12, 1966
Ink, graphite, and opaque white over
graphite underdrawing on layered paper
Published in the *Washington Post* (64)
LC-USZ62-127091

Fiddler, July 25, 1967
Ink, graphite, and opaque white over
graphite underdrawing on layered paper
Published in the *Washington Post* (65)
LC-USZ62-127090

*For long-lasting deep-down comfort smoke
Carcinos, with the special filter made from
a rabbit's foot,* September 3, 1967
Ink, graphite, and opaque white over
graphite underdrawing on layered paper
Published in the *Washington Post* (66)
LC-USZ62-127081

*"We'll let the overcoat out all the way,
and the robe will hardly show at all,"*
February 11, 1968
Ink, graphite, and opaque white over
graphite underdrawing on layered paper
Copyright 1968, Herblock,
The Washington Post (67)
LC-USZ62-127082

"She might have invaded Russia,"
September 3, 1968
Ink, graphite, and opaque white over
graphite underdrawing on layered paper
Published in the *Washington Post* (68)
LC-USZ62-127086

*"You see, the reason we're in Indochina is
to protect us boys in Indochina,"* May 5, 1970
Ink, graphite, and opaque white over
graphite underdrawing on layered paper
Published in the *Washington Post* (70)
LC-USZ62-126931

"I am Not a Crook"

Taped, January 18, 1970
Ink, graphite, and opaque white over
graphite underdrawing on layered paper
Published in the *Washington Post* (69)
LC-USZ62-126927

New figure on the American scene,
June 20, 1971
Reproduction of original drawing
Published in the *Washington Post* (71)

*For the championship of the United
States,* November 17, 1971
Ink, graphite, and opaque white over
graphite underdrawing on layered paper
Published in the *Washington Post* (72)
LC-USZ62-126926

"Now, as I was saying four years ago—",
August 9, 1972
Ink, graphite, and opaque white over
graphite underdrawing on layered paper
Published in the *Washington Post* (73)
LC-USZ62-126919

*"There's no need for an independent
investigation—We have everything well
in hand,"* September 8, 1972
Ink, graphite, and opaque white over
graphite underdrawing on layered paper
Published in the *Washington Post* (74)
LC-USZ62-126916

[Nixon awash in his office], June 26, 1973
Ink, graphite, and opaque white over
graphite underdrawing on paper
Published in the *Washington Post* (76)
LC-USZ62-126918

*"Move over—We can't stay in a holding
pattern forever,"* July 29, 1973
Ink, graphite, and opaque white over
graphite underdrawing on paper
Published in the *Washington Post* (77)
LC-USZ62-126920

[Nixon, with a money-bag for a face, carries a sign, "I am not a crook"], April 4, 1974
Ink, graphite, and opaque white over graphite underdrawing on paper
Published in the *Washington Post* (78)
LC-USZ62-126921

[I am not a crook], May 24, 1974
Reproduction of original drawing
Published in the *Washington Post* (79)

[Nixon, "unindicted co-conspirator"], July 14, 1974
Reproduction of original drawing
Published in the *Washington Post* (80)

One Nation, Indivisible

"Remember—don't vote for anyone who would interfere with the way we've been handling things," October 30, 1974
Ink, graphite, and opaque white over graphite underdrawing on paper
Published in the *Washington Post* (81)
LC-USZ62-126922

". . . One nation . . . indivisible . . . ," February 22, 1977
Ink, graphite, and opaque white, with tonal film overlay and porous point pen over graphite underdrawing on paper
Published in the *Washington Post* (83)
LC-USZ62-126888

"Read me what it says, Dad," June 8, 1977
Ink, crayon, and opaque white over blue pencil underdrawing on paper
Published in the *Washington Post* (84)
LC-USZ62-126885

"This here country ain't big enough for both of us," July 27, 1977
Ink, graphite, and opaque white over graphite underdrawing on paper
Published in the *Washington Post* (85)
LC-USZ62-126936

"Except for those of us who are above it," November 2, 1977
Ink, graphite, porous point pen, and opaque white over graphite underdrawing on paper
Published in the *Washington Post* (86)
LC-USZ62-126884

"We rub these sticks together till we strike a spark . . . we keep rubbing these sticks together . . . we take these sticks . . . ," February 1, 1978
Ink, graphite, crayon, porous point pen, opaque white, and overlays over graphite underdrawing on paper
Published in the *Washington Post* (87)
LC-USZ62-126886

"Ah, Independence Day—The glorious Fourth! Do see that the natives get a nice fireworks display," June 30, 1978
Ink, graphite, crayon, porous point pen, opaque white, and overlays over blue pencil underdrawing on paper
Published in the *Washington Post* (89)
LC-USZ62-126934

Moscow Olympics 1980, July 19, 1978
Ink, graphite, crayon, porous point pen, and opaque white, over graphite and blue pencil underdrawing on paper
Published in the *Washington Post* (90)
LC-USZ62-126929

Spiritual leader, April 8, 1979
Ink, crayon, porous point pen, opaque white, and overlays over blue pencil underdrawing on paper
Published in the *Washington Post* (91)
LC-USZ62-126933

"Rosalynn, it's him again," September 12, 1979
Ink, graphite, crayon, porous point pen, and opaque white, over blue pencil underdrawing on paper
Published in the *Washington Post* (92)
LC-USZ62-126932

Invasion of the Corporate Body Snatchers

Mined area, January 2, 1980
Ink, crayon, porous point pen, opaque white, and overlays over blue pencil underdrawing on paper
Published in the *Washington Post* (93)
LC-USZ62-126880

"You can do a favor for me—Rub out any gun control legislation," August 7, 1980
Ink, crayon, porous point pen, and opaque white, over blue pencil underdrawing on paper
Published in the *Washington Post* (94)
LC-USZ62-126877

"The Gods are angry," April 12, 1981
Ink, graphite, crayon, porous point pen, opaque white, and overlays over blue pencil underdrawing on paper
Published in the *Washington Post* (95)
LC-USZ62-126878

"On to Central America!" March 13, 1984
Ink, crayon, porous point pen, opaque white, and overlays over blue pencil underdrawing on paper
Published in the *Washington Post* (96)
LC-USZ62-126873

Invasion of the corporate body snatchers, April 21, 1985
Ink, crayon, porous point pen, opaque white, and overlay over blue pencil underdrawing on paper
Published in the *Washington Post* (97)
LC-USZ62-126883

"Right up my alley," July 19, 1985
Ink, crayon, porous point pen, opaque white, and overlays over blue pencil underdrawing on paper
Published in the *Washington Post* (98)
LC-USZ62-126872

Arms payoff for hostage release, November 11, 1986
Ink, crayon, porous point pen, opaque white, tonal film overlay, and overlay over blue pencil underdrawing on paper
Published in the *Washington Post* (99)
LC-USZ62-126881

"Speak softly and carry a big stick," December 21, 1986
Ink, crayon, porous point pen, opaque white, and overlay over blue pencil underdrawing on paper
Published in the *Washington Post* (100)
LC-USZ62-126879

"Our bags are packed"—Weinberger on Star Wars program, January 25, 1987
Ink, crayon, porous point pen, opaque white, and overlays over blue pencil underdrawing on paper
Published in the *Washington Post* (101)
LC-USZ62-126882

Church of the Heavenly Antenna, March 26, 1987
Ink, crayon, porous point pen, and opaque white,
over blue pencil underdrawing on paper
Published in the *Washington Post* (103)
LC-USZ62-126875

*"And we pray that you sinners out there
will see the light,"* May 3, 1987
Ink, crayon, porous point pen, and opaque
white, over blue pencil underdrawing on paper
Published in the *Washington Post* (104)
LC-USZ62-126871

"People's Republic," June 6, 1989
Ink, crayon, porous point pen, and opaque
white, over blue pencil underdrawing on paper
Published in the *Washington Post* (105)
LC-USZ62-126876

The Sorcerer's Apprentice

The sorcerer's apprentice, October 7, 1990
Ink, crayon, porous point pen, opaque white, and
overlay over blue pencil underdrawing on paper
Published in the *Washington Post* (106)
LC-USZ62-126892

Health coverage, May 3, 1991
Ink, crayon, porous point pen, opaque white, and
overlay over blue pencil underdrawing on paper
Published in the *Washington Post* (107)
LC-USZ62-126890

Economic-political currency, November 1, 1992
Ink, crayon, porous point pen, opaque white, and
overlays over blue pencil underdrawing on paper
Published in the *Washington Post* (109)
LC-USZ62-126891

Not Negroes! Not women! Not gays!
January 28, 1993
Ink, crayon, porous point pen, and opaque
white, over blue pencil underdrawing on paper
Published in the *Washington Post* (110)
LC-USZ62-126893

The daily sacrifices, October 1, 1993
Ink, crayon, porous point pen, opaque white, and
overlays over blue pencil underdrawing on paper
Published in the *Washington Post* (111)
LC-USZ62-126914

"What—Us tell fibs of some kind?" March 3, 1996
Ink, crayon, porous point pen, opaque white, and
overlays over blue pencil underdrawing on paper
Published in the *Washington Post* (112)
LC-USZ62-126915

*"True, I had coffee with those big contributors,
but I didn't swallow,"* October 9, 1997
Ink, crayon, porous point pen, opaque white, and
overlays over blue pencil underdrawing on paper
Published in the *Washington Post* (113)
LC-USZ62-126889

*"What have we got that's more like a close
shave?"* November 27, 1998
Ink, crayon, porous point pen, opaque white, and
overlays over blue pencil underdrawing on paper
Published in the *Washington Post* (115)
LC-USZ62-126912

Impeachment parade, January 10, 1999
Ink, crayon, porous point pen, opaque white, and
overlays over blue pencil underdrawing on paper
Published in the *Washington Post* (116)
LC-USZ62-126913

Lines in the Sand

Lines in the sand, February 26, 1999
Ink, crayon, porous point pen, opaque white, and
overlays over blue pencil underdrawing on paper
Published in the *Washington Post* (117)
LC-USZ62-126896

*Speakers on behalf of the Kosovo massacred
and homeless,* March 25, 1999
Ink, crayon, porous point pen, opaque white, and
overlays over blue pencil underdrawing on paper
Published in the *Washington Post* (137)
LC-USZ62-127455

*"Kids these days! Craziness in schools movies,
video games—terrible! Here—Try this dandy!"*
April 28, 1999
Ink, crayon, porous point pen, opaque white, and
overlays over blue pencil underdrawing on paper
Published in the *Washington Post* (118)
LC-USZ62-126898

Crime and punishment, November 5, 1999
Ink, crayon, porous point pen, opaque white, and
overlays over blue pencil underdrawing on paper
Published in the *Washington Post* (121)
LC-USZ62-126897

*"I don't know where your socks are, and if you
keep coming in here with that cigar I'm going
to call OSHA,"* January 5, 2000
Ink, crayon, porous point pen, opaque white, and
overlays over blue pencil underdrawing on paper
Published in the *Washington Post* (122)
LC-USZ62-126923

*"Just gunsmoke—For a moment I thought somebody
somewhere might be burning a flag,"* March 29, 2000
Ink, crayon, porous point pen, opaque white, and
overlays over blue pencil underdrawing on paper
Published in the *Washington Post* (124)
LC-USZ62-126925

*"Put this on—You're obviously not covered by
the First Amendment,"* March 31, 2000
Ink, crayon, porous point pen, opaque white, and
overlays over blue pencil underdrawing on paper
Published in the *Washington Post* (125)
LC-USZ62-126930

*"This must be that strange creature they mentioned
in history class,"* April 6, 2000
Ink, crayon, porous point pen, opaque white, and
overlays over blue pencil underdrawing on paper
Published in the *Washington Post* (126)
LC-USZ62-126928

Greatest country on earth, July 23, 2000
Ink, crayon, porous point pen, opaque white, and
overlays over blue pencil underdrawing on paper
Published in the *Washington Post* (153)
LC-USZ62-127444

Hare and Tortoise 2000

The pre-primary vote, June 11, 1999
Ink, crayon, porous point pen, opaque white, and
overlays over blue pencil underdrawing on paper
Published in the *Washington Post* (119)
LC-USZ62-126899

"Said Alice . . .'It's the stupidest tea-party
I ever was at in all my life," October 31, 1999
Ink, crayon, porous point pen, opaque white,
and overlays over blue pencil underdrawing
on paper
Published in the *Washington Post* (120)
LC-USZ62-126894

"'A house divided'—'Preserve the Union'—
when does he get to the important thing—
telling us all about his personal religion?"
February 10, 2000
Ink, crayon, porous point pen, opaque
white, and overlays over blue pencil
underdrawing on paper
Published in the *Washington Post* (123)
LC-USZ62-126924

"It's still a representative form of government—
they represent us," May 18, 2000
Ink, crayon, porous point pen, opaque
white, and overlays over blue pencil
underdrawing on paper
Published in the *Washington Post* (138)
LC-USZ62-127456

Hare and Tortoise 2000, June 18, 2000
Ink, crayon, porous point pen, opaque
white, and overlays over blue pencil
underdrawing on paper
Published in the *Washington Post* (139)
LC-USZ62-127457

Blaze Congress, Stripper, June 30, 2000
Ink, crayon, porous point pen, opaque
white, and overlays over blue pencil
underdrawing on paper
Published in the *Washington Post* (142)
LC-USZ62-127452

*I made my decision after listening
to Gore,* July 19, 2000
Ink, crayon, porous point pen, opaque
white, and overlays over blue pencil
underdrawing on paper
Published in the *Washington Post* (136)
LC-USZ62-127454

*Dick and Dad will tell me all I need to
know,* July 27, 2000
Ink, crayon, porous point pen, opaque
white, and overlays over blue pencil
underdrawing on paper
Published in the *Washington Post* (140)
LC-USZ62-127458

Jump Start, August 9, 2000
Ink, crayon, porous point pen, opaque white,
and overlays over blue pencil underdrawing
on paper
Published in the *Washington Post* (141)
LC-USZ62-127453

Caricatures of Herblock

[Herblock painting McCarthy, Nixon,
Reagan, and Clinton]
Ink and porous point pen on paper
Gift of Tony Auth (144)
LC-USZ62-127450

Herblock
Ink over graphite underdrawing
on layered paper
Gift of Jim Borgman (131)
LC-USZ62-127438

[Herblock as George Washington]
Porous point pen over graphite
underdrawing on paper
Gift of Paul and Kay Conrad (127)
LC-USZ62-127334

Herb's Real Close Shaves
Ink and porous point pen over
graphite underdrawing on paper
Gift of Jeff Danziger (133)
LC-USZ62-127440

[Herblock]
Porous point pen and crayon on paper
Gift of Jules Feiffer (149)
LC-USZ62-127448

[Herblock holding ink bottle with
Clinton's head popping out of it]
Ink and white-out over graphite
underdrawing on layered paper
Gift of Jack Higgins (128)
LC-USZ62-127435

Herblock is the greatest man in the world
Photocopy and photo lithograph print with
overlays and pencil on paper
Gift of Chuck Jones (152)
LC-USZ62-127445

The award-winning original Herb dressing
Color laserjet print on salad dressing bottle
Gift of Lynn Johnston (150)
LC-USZ62-127447 (recto)
LC-USZ62-127443 (verso)

Herb with famous early cartoon skewering Lincoln
Ink and porous point pen with opaque white over
graphite underdrawing with
paste-on on paper
Gift of Mike Luckovich (134)
LC-USZ62-127441

And they built the newspaper around him
Charcoal over watercolor on paper
Gift of Pat Oliphant (129)
LC-USZ62-127436

Herblock
Porous point pen and opaque white on paper
Gift of Mike Peters (148)
LC-USZ62-127449

This guy isn't recording history . . .
this guy is making history
Ink and white out over graphite
underdrawing with overlay on
duoshade paper
Gift of Joel Pett (151)
LC-USZ62-127446

[Herblock preparing to give Nixon a close shave]
Ink over blue pencil underdrawing
on layered paper
Gift of Ann Telnaes (130)
LC-USZ62-127437

[Herblock as a balloon above Earth]
Ink over graphite underdrawing on paper
Gift of Tom Toles (132)
LC-USZ62-127439

Herblock: The Official Chronology
Ink and porous point pen on layered paper
Gift of Signe Wilkinson (143)
LC-USZ62-127451

SELECT BIBLIOGRAPHY

The Herblock Book: Text and Cartoons by Herbert Block. Boston: Beacon Press, 1952.

Herblock's Here and Now. New York: Simon and Schuster, 1955.

Herblock's Special for Today. New York: Simon and Schuster, 1958.

Straight Herblock. New York: Simon and Schuster, 1964.

The Herblock Gallery. New York: Simon and Schuster, 1968.

Herblock's State of the Union. New York: Simon and Schuster, 1972.

Herblock Special Report. New York: Norton, 1974.

Herblock on All Fronts: Text and Cartoons. New York: New American Library, 1980.

Herblock through the Looking Glass. New York: Norton, 1984.

Herblock at large: "Let's Go Back a Little . . ." and Other Cartoons with Commentary. New York: Pantheon Books, 1987.

Herblock: A Cartoonist's Life. New York: Macmillan Pub., 1993.

Bella and Me: Life in the Service of a Cat. Chicago: Bonus Books, 1995.

Web Sites

On Politics—The Latest Herblock
http://washingtonpost.com/wp-srv/
politics/herblock/herblock.htm

On Politics—Herblock Archive
http://washingtonpost.com/wp-srv/
politics/herblock/archives.htm

On Politics—Five Decades of Herblock
http://washingtonpost.com/wp-srv/
politics/herblock/5decades.htm

Catalog records for works by Herbert Block and other related graphic works in the Library's collections are accessible from the Prints and Photographs Division Home Page: http://www.loc.gov/rr/print/ and from the Caroline and Irwin Swann Foundation for Caricature and Cartoon Home Page: http://lcweb.loc.gov/rr/print/swann/swannhome.html

CREDITS

Prints and Photographs Division
Harry Katz, *Curator*
Sara W. Duke, *Assistant Curator*
Lucia J. Rather, *Editorial and Research Assistance*

Interpretive Programs Office
Irene Chambers, *Interpretive Programs Officer*
Martha Hopkins, *Exhibit Director*
Deborah Durbeck, *Production Officer*
Margaret Brown, Registrar, Gwynn Wilhelm, Denise Agee, Pamela Steele, Tambra Johnson, Christopher O'Connor, Antonio LaGreca, and Ken Stoken

Conservation Office
Maria Nugent, Doris Hamburg, Louise Condon, Holly Krueger, Kate Morrison Soyeon Choi, Beatriz Haspo, Sylvia Albro, Ann Grossman, Linda Stiber Morenus, Heather Wanser, Terry Boone, Yasmeen Khan, Hans Wang, Kaare Chaffe, Sonja Reid, and Ann Seibert.

ITS Scan Lab
Lynn Brooks, Domenic Sergi, Michael Smallwood, and Jade Curtis

Photoduplication Service
Yusef El Amin

Exhibition and Publication Design
Riggs Ward Design

The Library of Congress wishes to acknowledge the valuable contributions of Herbert Block, Jean Rickard, Marcela Brané, and Sarah Armstrong to the preparation and planning of this exhibition.

The Library of Congress is grateful to the following artists contributing original works in honor of Herbert Block to the exhibition and permanent collections: Tony Auth, Jim Borgman, Paul Conrad, Jeff Danziger, Jules Feiffer, Jack Higgins, Lynn Johnston, Chuck Jones, Mike Luckovich, Pat Oliphant, Mike Peters, Joel Pett, Ann Telnaes, Tom Toles, and Signe Wilkinson.

The exhibition and catalogue were prepared with funds provided by the Caroline and Erwin Swann Memorial Fund for Caricature and Cartoon. The Swann Fund supports an ongoing program at the Library of Congress of preservation, publication, exhibition, acquisition, and scholarly research in the related fields of cartoon, caricature, and illustration.

REPRODUCTION NUMBER(S): Library of Congress reproduction numbers, beginning with the prefix "LC-USZ," are provided here for the reader's convenience in obtaining black-and-white photographs ("LC-USZ62-****") or color transparencies ("LC-USZC4-****") from the Library's Photoduplication Service. Reproduction of works in this catalogue is restricted by copyright law.